DANGEROUS DINOSAURS
DINOSAURS
AND THE PREHISTORIC
WORLD

Liz Miles

W
FRANKLIN WATTS
LONDON · SYDNEY

First published in 2015 by Franklin Watts

Copyright © Arcturus Holdings Limited

Franklin Watts
338 Euston Road
London
NW1 3BH

Franklin Watts Australia
Level 17/207 Kent Street, Sydney, NSW 2000

Produced by Arcturus Publishing Limited,
26/27 Bickels Yard, 151–153 Bermondsey Street, London SE1 3HA

Author: Liz Miles
Editors: Joe Harris, Alex Woolf and Joe Fullman
Designer: Emma Randall
Original design concept: Notion Design

Picture Credits:
Key: b-bottom, m-middle, l-left, r-right, t-top
All images by pixel-shack.com except for:
Shutterstock: p20 b, p21 t, p21 b, p22 b, p27 b.
Wikipedia Commons: p23 b.

A CIP catalogue record for this book is available from the British Library.

Dewey Decimal Classification Number: 567.9
ISBN: 978 1 4451 4157 2

Printed in China

Franklin Watts is a division of Hachette Children's Books, an Hachette
UK company.
www.hachette.co.uk

SL004433UK

Supplier 03, Date 1214, Print Run 3759

CONTENTS

DINOSAUR PLANET

The dinosaurs were a group of reptiles that ruled the Earth for over 160 million years. They ranged from giant hunters, such as Spinosaurus (SPINE-oh-SORE-us) to tiny speedsters, like Compsognathus (comp-sog-NATH-us).

Plant-eating dinosaurs were in constant danger from savage meat-eaters. Some dinosaurs, like hadrosaurs (HAD-roh-sores), roamed in herds. Others, like Euoplocephalus (YOU-oh-plo-SEFF-ah-luss) were most likely solitary.

Dinosaurs lived at different periods. Some of the best known and most frightening dinosaurs, such as the fearsome hunter Tyrannosaurus rex (tie-RAN-oh-SORE-us REX), and the horned Triceratops (try-SEH-rah-tops), stalked the Earth during the Cretaceous period.

An asteroid streaks through the sky toward Earth where it will wipe out the dinosaurs.

OTHER PREHISTORIC MONSTERS

The dinosaurs may have ruled the land, but they were not the only creatures to call the prehistoric Earth their home. They lived alongside insects, mammals and other reptiles.

During the dinosaur era, terrifying pterosaurs (flying lizards) ruled the skies, while the oceans were filled with fantastical sea monsters – aggressive reptiles, monstrous squid and giant sharks.

Then, mysteriously, about 65 million years ago, all the dinosaurs, together with many other creatures, suddenly died out.

CHANGING EARTH

THE STORY OF OUR DYNAMIC PLANET

RED-HOT PLANET

Four and a half billion years ago, Earth had no land, oceans, atmosphere or life. Pounded by meteorites, it became hotter and hotter until most of it was molten. But slowly, gas from inside leaked out and an atmosphere formed. About 3.8 billion years ago, oceans began to appear.

DAWN OF LIFE

About 3.5 billion years ago, most of Earth's surface was a vast, shallow ocean. It was here that the first simple, single-celled life forms emerged. More complex, multi-celled life wouldn't evolve for another two billion years.

Earth today is very different from the place where dinosaurs once roamed. Our world may seem unchanging, but it is in fact in a constant state of gradual change. The planet's surface is made up of huge plates that float on a mass of molten (liquid) rock. Over millions of years, the plates slowly move, causing continents to shift, mountains to rise and oceans to grow and shrink. Fossils show us that the land masses were arranged very differently in prehistoric times.

AGE OF THE DINOSAURS

Land masses slowly emerged. When the dinosaurs first appeared about 225 million years ago (in the Triassic period) all the continents were one giant land mass, or 'supercontinent'. By the time the dinosaurs died out (at the end of the Cretaceous period, 65 million years ago), the land had split up into continents that look familiar to us today.

THE MODERN WORLD

Today's Earth is still changing. The continents are still moving, species are becoming extinct and new species are evolving.

TIMELINE

OF LIFE ON EARTH

Scientists have divided the billions of years of prehistoric time into periods. Dinosaurs lived in the Triassic, Cretaceous and Jurassic periods, while modern humans evolved in the Quaternary period.

← **CAMBRIAN**
541–485 mya:
Life forms become
more complex.

↓ **SILURIAN**
443–419 mya:
First creatures on land.

↑ **ORDOVICIAN**
485–443 mya:
Arthropods (creatures with
exoskeletons)
rule the seas. Plants
colonise the land.

↑ **PRECAMBRIAN**
4,570–541 million years ago
(mya): The first life forms
appear. They are tiny, one-
celled creatures.

↑ **DEVONIAN**
419–359 mya: First insects,
fish now dominate the seas.

↓ CRETACEOUS

145–65 mya: Spinosaurus and T. rex evolve. Dinosaur extinction.

↘ QUATERNARY

2.6 mya– today: Woolly mammoths roam the Earth, modern humans evolve.

← PALEOGENE/ NEOGENE

65–2.6 mya: Many giant mammal species emerge

↓ TRIASSIC

252–201 mya: First dinosaurs.

↑ JURASSIC

201–145 mya: The largest plant-eating dinosaurs evolve.

↑ TODAY

← PERMIAN

299–252 mya: First therapsids (ancestors of mammals) evolve.

← CARBONIFEROUS

359–299 mya: Reptiles first appear, vast forests cover the land.

UNDERWATER CREATURES

The ancient seas teemed with life millions of years before the dinosaurs stalked the land. The first creatures to live in the oceans were single-celled life forms. They were followed by strange, multi-celled organisms. These gradually evolved into scary-looking marine creatures that crept, burrowed and hunted for food.

TOP PREDATOR

Anomalocaris (A-nom-ah-lo-CA-ris), which means 'abnormal shrimp', was a large and dangerous predator. It searched for prey with its two compound eyes (each with thousands of lenses) on stalks. Up to 2 m (6 ft) long, it would have been a terrifying sight. The mouth was made of crushing plates that surrounded cutting prongs. Spiked arms around the mouth would have captured its prey, and pulled it down into its barbed throat.

FIVE-EYED MONSTER

The palm-sized Opabinia (OH-pa-BIN-ee-ah) had five eyes and lived in Cambrian seas. It may also have spent a lot of time burrowing into the mud on the seabed to hunt for worms. Its long proboscis (an organ extending from its face) had grasping spines.

MYSTERIOUS SEAS

Between 635 and 545 million years ago, animal life developed from single-celled forms to soft-bodied, multi-celled forms. We don't know much about the first sea creatures. As they had no hard shells or skeletons, only a few fossils survive. Many may have looked like soft blobs, or similar to today's marine worms, jellyfish and sea pens.

 # TIME DETECTIVES

Marine fossils usually come from creatures that had shells, skeletons or exoskeletons. Ancient seabeds are sometimes uncovered when rivers cut through old rock (as in the Grand Canyon, USA). Scientists can work out the age of fossils by the layer of rock they are found in — the deeper they are buried, the more ancient they are.

EMERGING ONTO THE LAND

Fish slowly ventured onto the land, evolving the body features of amphibians, such as lungs to breathe and four legs to help them move. No one knows why some went ashore – perhaps it was to escape from hungry arthropods, or maybe they got stuck in pools that were drying out.

The first fish-like land creatures may have flopped ashore in the Devonian period. They would have dragged themselves about on adapted fins, like today's mudskippers. True, four-legged amphibians like Eryops (EH-ree-ops) developed later.

OPEN WIDE!

About 290 million years ago, Eryops lurked in the waters – a huge, sturdy amphibian and one of the top predators of Permian times. It had no chewing teeth but did have wide-opening jaws. It must have grasped its prey and perhaps tossed it in the air until it was dead, using special teeth in the roof of its mouth. It would then have swallowed the creature whole, like a crocodile.

MUD FLOPPER

Ichthyostega (IK-thee-oh-STAY-gah) lived before Eryops, in late Devonian times. It was a weird mix of fish and amphibian. It had a fin at the end of its tail, but also had leg and toe bones. The hind legs were used like paddles, and the front limbs were probably strong enough to allow it to drag itself onto the shore and flop about on the mud like a modern-day mudskipper. It had lungs that would have allowed it to breathe air for short stretches of time.

TIME DETECTIVES

As fish fin prints and four-legged amphibian footprints look very different, fossil footprints are an important clue to help us find out when creatures first emerged from the water. Fossilised footprints with toes from 395 million years ago were found in Poland and are thought to be the oldest evidence of amphibians walking on the land.

EARLY REPTILES

FIERCE FORERUNNERS

Over time, the climate became drier. The vast, swampy forests of the Carboniferous period disappeared. The amphibians suffered because they needed to lay their eggs in water. Some, however, evolved into reptiles, which thrived because they could lay their eggs on land.

Early reptiles included fish-eaters with deadly teeth, like Ophiacodon (oh-fee-ACK-oh-don). Some, like Dimetrodon (die-MET-roe-don), which emerged later, had spectacular sails growing from their backs.

SNAKE TOOTH

Ophiacodon, which means 'snake tooth', was one of the earliest land-based reptiles. It lived in late Carboniferous and early Permian times, and probably spent a lot of time in water, grabbing fish with its mass of tiny, sharp teeth. It probably hunted down amphibians on shore, too, including its smaller, plant-eating cousin, Edaphosaurus (eh-DAFF-oh-SORE-us). Around 3.4 m (11 ft) long, Ophiacodon was a top hunter with a powerful bite, and its only challengers were other Ophiacodons.

FIN BACK

Dimetrodon was a fierce carnivore that hunted the land for its prey 50 million years before the dinosaurs appeared. It was the biggest and probably the most aggressive creature of its time. No one knows exactly what the sail on its back was for. It might have been used to threaten competitors, and to store heat from the sun for when it was cold. On hot days it might have been used like a car radiator, to cool the creature down.

VITAL STATISTICS

DIMETRODON

Meaning of name: Two shapes of teeth

Family: Sphenacodontidae

Period: Early Permian

Size:
1.7-4.6 m / 5.6-15.1 ft length

Weight: up to 250 kg / 550 lb

Distinguishing feature:
Large, thin sail on back

Diet: Meat and insects

SAIL AWAY
Skin covered spines grew from Dimetrodon's backbone to form a sail.

QUICK MOVER
Its legs, which spread out from either side of its body, allowed it to move fast. The amphibians and reptiles it preyed on probably found it hard to escape.

FLESH-EATER
It had two types of teeth – sharp and serrated. The serrated teeth were like meat knives, ideal for tearing the flesh from its catch.

THE FIRST DINOSAURS

HUNGRY HUNTERS

Dinosaurs evolved from reptiles, and first appeared in Triassic times. The earliest dinosaurs already had many of the deadly features of the later, more famous meat-eaters. They had curved finger claws, sharp teeth and jaws built to hold onto prey struggling to escape.

FIRST FOSSIL FINDS

Fossils of the earliest dinosaurs, such as Eoraptor (EE-owe-RAP-tore), have been found in Argentina. But they were not all top predators – the meat-eating Herrerasaurus (herr-RARE-oh-SORE-us), for example, may have itself been the prey of a bigger monster.

DAWN RAIDER

Although an early dinosaur, the fox-sized Eoraptor looked very much like the hunting dinosaurs of Jurassic times, millions of years later. It walked upright on two legs and had meat-eating jaws. Its teeth were razor sharp, small and backward-curving, so could give a nasty bite. Its name means 'dawn plunderer'.

LONG IN THE TOOTH

Herrerasaurus was 5 m (16.5 ft) tall, with teeth more than twice as long as a human's and grooved like a saw for cutting. It was also equipped with sharp claws at the end of its three-fingered hands. A good sense of hearing may have helped it to find its prey, and also to listen out for an aggressor that shared the same territories: a giant crocodile-like carnivore called Saurosuchus (sore-oh-SOO-kuss).

EARLY PLANT-CHOMPER

One of the first plant-eating dinosaurs was Thecodontosaurus (thee-co-DON-toe-SORE-us), which had small, plant-cutting teeth and walked on all fours. It was as tall as an adult human and chomped away at low-growing plants.

AGE OF THE DINOSAURS

Dinosaurs ruled the world for 150 million years. The Age of the Dinosaurs covered the Triassic, Jurassic and Cretaceous periods, together called the therozoic era.

The dinosaurs ranged from giant-sized to chicken-sized, and from aggressive meat-eaters to gentle, grazing plant-eaters. No land was safe from the dinosaurs – their fossils have been found on every continent, and they lived in many varied habitats, from wetlands to arid open plains, and from coastlines and lagoons to forests and deserts.

CAVERN-JAWED KILLERS

The theropods (THAIR-oh-pods) were vicious, two-legged carnivores. They included Giganotosaurus (JIG-an-OH-toe-SORE-us) and T. rex, shown here. Their jaws were huge, even compared with the head of a large sauropod like Amargasaurus (ah-MAR-gah-SORE-us). Giganotosaurus probably hunted in packs, and together would have been capable of bringing down the mighty Amargasaurus, despite the herbivore's defensive whipping tail and spiny back.

DINOSAUR DETECTIVES

A complete or near-complete fossil of a dinosaur skeleton is a rare but important find, so it has to be excavated with care. The position of each fossil bone is recorded before it is removed. Scientists then get to work reconstructing the dinosaur. Missing pieces are filled in with plaster.

LAND GIANTS

The sauropods – the heaviest, tallest and longest animals ever to pound the Earth – lived on plants. Their tree trunk-like legs and long, stretching necks allowed them to reach high-growing plants, and their colossal size and whip-like tails intimidated the killers that stalked them. The sauropods included Apatosaurus (a-PAT-oh-SORE-us), which was four times taller than a modern giraffe.

PROTECTED BY PLATES

Plant-eaters developed ways of protecting themselves from meat-eaters. Ankylosaurus (ANK-ill-oh-SORE-us), for example, was covered in thick, bony plates, as well as spikes and studs, to shield it from the bites of hungry carnivores. It also had a clubbed tail to thwack at hunters.

DINO DIETS

Dinosaurs grazed on plants (herbivores), chomped through meat (carnivores) or ate both plants and meat (omnivores). Their fossilised skeletons, especially the teeth, are evidence of what they ate. Occasionally, the remains of a dinosaur's last meal are found, such as a pterosaur bone in the guts of a Velociraptor.

ALLOSAURUS (AL-oh-SORE-us) →
was one of the most common meat-eaters.

IGUANODON (ig-you-AH-noh-don)
was a typical plant-eater.

LEGS AND ELBOWS
Iguanodon walked on all fours but could also lean back on its hind legs to reach higher vegetation. The elbows on its fore-limbs allowed it to bend low for low-growth grazing.

BEAKY MOUTH
Iguanodon's toothless beak was perfect for cutting through vegetation. Back teeth on the top jaw closed down inside the teeth at the bottom, so they worked like scissors. Cheeks meant their food did not spill out while they chewed.

FLEXIBLE FINGER
The smallest finger was bendy and could curve around a high branch. Iguanodon could then tug the branch down to get to leaves at the top, which would otherwise be out of reach.

CLAWED FOR THE CATCH

Powerful arms, each ending in three claws, may have allowed Allosaurus to hold its struggling prey tight, while aiming for a deadly bite on its soft throat.

CANNIBAL

Allosaurus jaws could open wide but were not as strong as some hunting dinosaurs. It may have fed on carrion as well as live prey. Fossil evidence suggests that it was even cannibalistic, feeding on the flesh of other Allosaurus.

FLESH-RIPPING TEETH

Allosaurus had teeth 5-10 cm (2-4 in) long, designed to saw chunks of flesh from its prey. The pointed teeth curved backwards, to stop prey escaping its grasp. An Allosaurus bite mark on a Stegosaurus (steg-oh-SORE-us) suggests that this was one of the dinosaurs it ate.

WATERING HOLE

We know from fossil evidence that herbivorous dinosaurs often travelled in herds, and some types of predators travelled in packs. Creatures of different species would have gathered together at watering holes, just like modern animals.

EXTINCTION EVENT

Sixty-five million years ago, the dinosaurs disappeared. Many other species also died out around this time, suggesting that a sudden catastrophe made it impossible for lots of animals to survive. This could have been an asteroid or comet, volcanic eruptions or a combination of both.

DUST CLOUDS

If a meteor hit Earth, the dust clouds would have been so thick they would have have blocked out the sun for months. Temperatures would have dropped, causing the widespread death of forests and animals.

DEEP IMPACT!

Some scientists believe that the dinosaurs died out after a giant comet or asteroid fell to Earth. It would have smashed into the Earth's crust, hurling tons of dust into the atmosphere.

VIOLENT VOLCANOES

Around the time the dinosaurs died out, there was a lot of volcanic activity in northern India. These volcanoes were emitting lava for thousands of years – the lava flows are estimated to have covered an area about half the size of India! The chemicals released from the eruptions would have had a worldwide impact, causing major changes in the Earth's atmosphere. Many scientists believe that volcanic eruptions were killing off the dinosaurs long before a comet or asteroid fell to Earth.

DINOSAUR DETECTIVES

The Chicxulub crater in Mexico, shown here in an artist's impression, provides evidence that a huge meteor impact took place. This massive crater is 180 km (112 miles) in width – the meteor that created it is thought to have been 10 km (6 miles) wide!

AFTER THE DINOSAURS

SAVAGE MAMMALS

After the dinosaurs, mammals grew to become the largest animals both on land and in the sea. They included the fearsome, curved-toothed Smilodon (SMILE-oh-don), which belonged to a family of now extinct cat-like creatures called machairodonts (mah-CARE-oh-donts).

Many mammals from the Paleogene, Neogene and Quaternary periods looked like species that are alive today, but terrifyingly enlarged. Some, such as Smilodon, lived up to the time when humans had evolved and may have even hunted humans for food.

DEADLY SMILE

Smilodon had a deadly bite – it could open its mouth twice as wide as a modern-day lion. As well as its biting teeth, including the two huge, curved canine teeth, it had chewing teeth at the back of its jaws. This hunter may have leapt from trees or the undergrowth to ambush its prey. It would then use its powerful body to wrestle its victim to the ground and hold it there with its huge front paws, ready for one precise and deadly bite.

LOOK OUT FOR THE TAIL

Doedicurus (DAY-dih-CORE-us) was an incredible mammal from the Quaternary period that must have looked a little like a giant (and terrifying) armadillo. Its protective shell was covered in skin and may have been hairy. Males swiped their tails armed with knobs or spikes at each other in power battles. Dents from the tails have been found on the shells of some males.

DOEDICURUS
VERSUS
ARMADILLO

	DOEDICURUS	GIANT ARMADILLO
HEIGHT	1.5 m (5 ft)	0.3 m (1 ft)
LENGTH	4 m (13 ft)	1.5 m (5 ft)
WEIGHT	Up to 2,370 kg (2.6 tons)	Up to 32 kg (71 lb)
TEETH	Grinding teeth at the back	80–100 peg-shaped teeth
FOOD	Plants	Insects, small animals, plants, fruit, carrion

DESCENDANTS OF THE DINOSAURS

The closest things to dinosaurs living on our planet today are birds. Modern birds have evolved from two-legged, meat-eating dinosaurs called theropods. Scientists found the evidence for this when they made an incredible discovery – fossilised dinosaurs that had feathers.

Species like Caudipteryx (caw-DIP-ter-ix), which possessed both dinosaur and bird features, show the gradual transition from one type of animal to the other. At first, feathers were just for warmth and display, but then, through evolution, they began to be used for flight, too. Perhaps the first true bird was Archaeopteryx (are-kee-OP-ter-ix), whose fossil was discovered in 1862. Even though Archaeopteryx was more bird than dinosaur, it could probably only flutter rather than fly.

SHOWTIME TAIL
Like birds today, Caudipteryx may have spread its tail feathers to attract mates or scare off predators.

DOWNY COAT
Its feather coating was for warmth, not flight. The downy covering might have been marked with tones and pigments, although we can't know for sure as these rarely survive in fossils.

BIRD-LEGS
Like a modern bird, the early Cretaceous Caudipteryx may have perched on branches or used its long legs to wade into lakes or rivers.

FLIGHTLESS
The feathers on the arms were too short and the wrong shape for flight. They may have been used to keep their young warm in their nests.

MAIDEN FLIGHT

With sharp teeth and a bony tail, Archaeopteryx was similar to a theropod. Yet it also had feathers and wings that allowed it to fly, although not as well as most birds today. To fly, it probably launched itself from trees or rocks.

DINOSAURS DOWN THE GARDEN

Of course there aren't really dinosaurs living in anyone's garden, yet there are incredible similarities between some birds today and the predatory little theropods of the Cretaceous period. Feathers, lightweight skulls, wishbones in their skeletons and two legs for walking are some of the shared features.

DINO WORLD

The first dinosaur fossil was found in 1676 and was thought to be from a human giant – the idea of massive reptiles was beyond the imagination. Since then, dinosaur fossils have been found on every continent. New types of dinosaurs are still being regularly discovered, breaking records and giving scientists a fuller picture of the dinosaur world.

TYRANNOSAURUS REX

FOUND IN: North America
WHEN IT LIVED: Late Cretaceous
(67 –65 million years ago)
The first fossils of a killer Tyrannosaurus rex were found in Wyoming, USA, in 1900.

HERRERASAURUS

FOUND IN: South America
WHEN IT LIVED: Late Triassic
(228 million years ago)
Herrerasaurus was named after the rancher Don Victorino Herrera, who found the first fossil in 1958 in Argentina.

SMILODON

FOUND IN: South America
WHEN IT LIVED: Pleistocene-Modern
(2 million to 10,000 years ago)
The first Smilodon fossils were found in caves in Brazil.

Dinosaur Height Guide

■ Human – 1.7m (5.6 ft) ■ Velociraptor – 1m (3.2 ft) ■ Triceratops – 3m (9.8 ft)
■ T. rex – 5.6m (18 ft) ■ Argentinosaurus – 8m (26.2 ft) height

ICHTHYOSTEGA

FOUND IN: Greenland
WHEN IT LIVED: Late Devonian (370 million years ago)
Ichthyostega was first discovered in Greenland in 1932. The creature was an important link between fish and the first backboned creatures to live on land.

THECODONTOSAURUS

FOUND IN: United Kingdom
WHEN IT LIVED: Late Triassic
(227-205 million years ago)
In 1834, a scientist and surgeon found the fossils of this early dinosaur.

IGUANODON

FOUND IN: Europe
WHEN IT LIVED:
Early Cretaceous
(140-110 million years ago)
It is thought that Mary Mantell, wife of an early fossl-hunter, found the first fossils of this duck-billed plant-eater in 1822.

CAUDIPTERYX

FOUND IN: China
WHEN IT LIVED:
Early Cretaceous
(125-122 million years ago)
The bird-like but flightless Caudipertyx was discovered in northeastern China in 1997.

DIMETRODON

FOUND IN: North America and Germany
WHEN IT LIVED: Permian (280 million years ago)
Dimetrodon was discovered in the late 1880s in North America. It was not until 2001 that Dimetrodon fossils were found outside America – in Germany.

DOEDICURUS

FOUND IN: South America
WHEN IT LIVED: Pleistocene-Modern (2 million-10,000 years ago)
Fossils of this huge, two-ton armadillo-like herbivore were first named in 1874. Its name means 'pestle-tail'.

GLOSSARY

arthropds An animal with an external skeleton, such as insects and spiders.

Carboniferous A prehistoric period when there were many swamps and forests. Fossil fuels later formed from the trees and plants that died.

carrion Flesh from a creature that has died, and a source of food for some birds and animals.

Cretaceous A prehistoric period during which mammals and giant dinosaurs lived, and which ended with the mass extinction of the dinosaurs 65 million years ago.

Devonian A prehistoric period, also known as the Age of Fishes, when the oceans were warm and filled with many types of evolving fish.

evolve To change gradually over time.

extinct Not existing anymore.

fossil The remains of a prehistoric organism preserved in rock.

fossilised Made into a fossil.

grazing Feeding on low-growing plants.

hadrosaurs Plant-eating family of dinosaurs, also known as duck-billed dinosaurs because of their beak-like mouths.

herbivore A plant-eater.

hibernating Spending the winter in a dormant (slowed-down or inactive) state.

Jurassic A prehistoric period in which many large dinosaurs lived. It is also called the Age of Reptiles.

mosasaur A giant, meat-eating, and sea-living family of reptiles that used four paddle-like limbs to swim.

omnivorous Eating a diet of both plants and meat.

predator An animal that hunts other animals to kill and eat.

prey An animal that is hunted by other animals for food.

reptiles Cold-blooded animals that usually lay eggs and have scales.

sauropods A group of giant, four-legged plant-eating dinosaurs with small heads, long necks and tails.

sea pen A sea animal similar to corals.

serrated Having a jagged, saw-like edge.

theropods A group of two-legged, meat-eating dinosaurs, ranging in size from small to very large.

Triassic A prehistoric period during which the first dinosaurs and mammals evolved.

FURTHER INFORMATION

FURTHER READING

Dinosaur Record Breakers by Darren Naish (Carlton Kids, 2014)

Dinosaurs: A Children's Encyclopedia by editors of DK (Dorling Kindersley, 2011)

Evolution Revolution by Robert Winston (Dorling Kindersley, 2009)

National Geographic Kids: The Ultimate Dinopedia by Don Lessem (National Geographic Society, 2012)

Prehistoric Safari: Giant Dinosaurs by Liz Miles (Franklin Watts, 2012)

The Usborne World Atlas of Dinosaurs by Susanna Davidson (Usborne Publishing, 2013)

WEBSITES

http://www.bbc.co.uk/nature/14343366
A regularly updated part of the BBC website, dedicated to dinosaurs. There is a news section and plenty of cool videos.

http://animals.nationalgeographic.com/animals/prehistoric/
This part of the National Geographic website is home to some fascinating articles about dinosaurs. There are also some excellent pictures.

www.nhm.ac.uk/kids-only/index.html
The young people's section of the Natural History Museum website. Packed with downloads, games, quizzes and lots of information about dinosaurs.

INDEX

SERIES CONTENTS

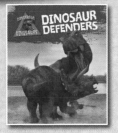

DINOSAUR DEFENDERS

Attack and Defence • Triceratops: Horn-Faced Fighter • Frightening Frills • Pachycephalosaurids: Butting Boneheads • Stegosaurus: Savage Spiker • Ankylosaurs: Defensive Demons • Hadrosaurs: Deafening Duckbills • Sauropods: Tail-Thrashing Titans • Patterns and Feathers • Herding Heavies • Danger Senses • Dino World • Timeline of Life on Earth

DINOSAUR RECORD-BREAKERS

Battling Giants • Titanosaurs: The Heavyweights • Smallest Dinosaurs • Ultimate Hunter: Spinosaurus • Deadliest Dinosaur • Skyscrapers • Dinosaur Egg Records • Fastest Dinosaurs • Longest Claws • Tough as Tanks: Best Protection • Smart Cookies or Bird Brains? • Famous Fossils • Timeline of Life on Earth

DINOSAURS AND THE PREHISTORIC WORLD

Dinosaur Planet • Changing Earth • Timeline of Life on Earth • Underwater Creatures • Emerging onto the Land • Early Reptiles: Fierce Forerunners • The First Dinosaurs: Hungry Hunters • Age of the Dinosaurs • Dino Diets • Extinction Event • After the Dinosaurs: Savage Mammals • Descendants of the Dinosaurs • Dino World

KILLER DINOSAURS

Ultimate Predators • Tyrant Lizard • Ravenous Giant • Utahraptor: Vicious Pack Hunter • Sickle-Clawed Runners • Carnotaurus: 'Flesh-Eating Bull' • Troodon: Night Tracker • Terrifying Teeth • Baryonyx: Fish Hunter • Packs and Families • Savage Killers or Just Scavengers? • Dino World • Timeline of Life on Earth

FLYING MONSTERS

Savage Skies • Needle-Toothed Terrors • Pteranodons: Awesome Axe-Heads • Jutting-Jawed Pterosaurs • Dimorphodon: Tooth-Beaked Hunter • Furry Fiends • Quetzalcoatlus: Giant Vulture • Crested Competitors • Keen Eyed Killers • Bird-Like Biters • Flying Families • Winged World • Timeline of Life on Earth

SEA MONSTERS

From the Deep • Shell Shock • Cameroceras: Tentacled Terror • Super-Sharks • Long-Necked Hunters • Liopleurodon: Jurassic Tyrant • Massive-Jawed Monsters • Ichthyosaurs: Fish-Lizards • Fearsome Fish • Giant Crocs • Changing Seas • Fossil Finds • Timeline of Life on Earth